Life is Tremendous!
CHARLIE JONES

TYNDALE HOUSE PUBLISHERS
Wheaton, Illinois

Cartoons by Wayne Stayskall

Library of Congress Catalog Card Number 68-31704
ISBN 8423-2200-0, Cloth; 8423-2201-9, Paper
Twenty-third printing, May 1979.
© 1968 Charles E. Jones. Printed in U.S.A.

Life is tremendous! It really is. You can be happy, involved, relevant, productive, healthy and secure in the midst of a high-pressure, commercialized, automated, pill-prone society. It's not easy nor automatic, but it's possible through the development of certain personal qualities which make up the traits of leadership. And you can be a leader, because leaders are made, not born. Are you ready for leadership? Whooooo, let's go!

Contents

I Guarantee

The reading of these pages will be one of the most profitable things you have ever done. How can I make such a guarantee? In the past twelve months I've shared these ideas with companies that together have exceeded $20 billion in sales. Many of these leading salesmen and executives have returned with their families to sit through the same three-hour lecture several times in a twelve-month period. Our mail from business-men, housewives, clergymen and college students reports the revolutionary effects of these ideas.

If you are to profit as countless thousands have, don't remember what I say here . . . that's right: *you must not remember what I say.* You wonder: "Aren't you going to say anything worth remembering?" Yes, I am, but the value of this book won't be in your remembering what I say but rather in remembering what you think as a result of what I say. My objective is to prove that what you think as a result of what I say is far more important than your remembering what I say.

I always start a lecture by asking everyone to refrain from writing down what I say because I believe that what you hear doesn't do you a great deal of good — if it did we'd all be a lot better than we are! We sure have heard plenty of instructions, tips, rules and suggestions, haven't we? I am stretching the point, but bear with me.

Coming out of a meeting one day, a man said to me, "Mr. Jones, I'll bet you that ten percent of these people can't remember ten percent of what you said ten minutes after you said it." He was right, and for that reason I have geared my talking and writing to getting you to remember what you think, and more than that to get you to think what you already know. My number one objective is to stir up your thought processes and help you frame your best thoughts with words so you can harness and use them. Concentrate on what you think from here on, and I guarantee a tremendously profitable adventure through practicing the Laws of Leadership.

We succeed in enterprises which demand the positive qualities we possess, but we excel in those which can also make use of our defects. — *Alexis de Tocqueville*

1

Leadership Is Learning
to Live

Leadership is an obligation and a privilege of every person, young and old, because it is based simply on what we do. Everyone is responsible for something that he alone must do. If we enjoy this privilege and discharge our obligation, we grow; if we ignore our opportunity, we join the shrinking violets of humanity. The most tremendous experience of life is the learning process. The saddest time is when a person thinks that he has learned enough.

Did you ever hear these famous last words: "This is one thing I've learned"? Know what he's learned? *Nothing!* I remember saying that, and soon afterward I would wind up learning all over again what I thought I had just learned. Now I've almost learned one thing, and that is that the process of learning to live is TREEE-

MENNNDOUS! We never stop growing until we stop learning, and people who are learning this simple truth will *grow* old but never get old.

Once a boy was rowing an oldtimer across a wide river. The oldtimer picked a floating leaf from the water, studied it for a moment and then asked the boy if he knew anything about biology. "No, I don't," the boy replied. The oldtimer said, "Son, you have missed twenty-five percent of your life."

As they rowed on, the oldtimer took a rock from the bottom of the boat. He turned it in his hand, studying its coloration, and asked the boy, "Son, do you know anything about geology?" The boy sheepishly replied, "No, I don't, sir." The oldtimer said, "Son, you've missed fifty percent of your life."

Twilight was approaching and the oldtimer gazed raptly at the North Star that had begun to twinkle. After a while he asked the boy, "Son, do you know anything about astronomy?" The boy, head bowed and brow furrowed, admitted: "No, I don't, sir." The oldtimer scolded: "Son, you've missed seventy-five percent of your life!"

Just then the boy noticed the huge dam upstream beginning to crumble and torrents of water pouring through the break. Quickly he turned to the oldtimer and shouted, "Sir, do you know how to swim?" The oldtimer replied, "No," to which the boy shouted back, *"You just lost your life."*

You need not learn all the methods and techniques of living, but you must be a real student of "learning to live" if you are *to lead dynamically*, because leadership is nothing more than really *LIVING*.

This book is really about you, not primarily the author. I may intrude here and there to show you a bad example to avoid, but the book will talk about *you*. It relates you to laws of living, which I call the Laws of Leadership. Anyone who is not leading others in life is not really living. Whether you realize it or not, other people lead you in every area of your life, for good or ill. And with every passing moment your own leadership responsibilities are increasing. The person who recognizes this will never be bored, but the person who forgets or ignores it will be dead long before his funeral. My son Jere once remarked that he was interested in life after death but even more in *life after birth*. We all should be interested in that!

No one lives unto himself. There is an "I-Land" and a "You-Land." The I-Land is a lonely place, and countless thousands are shipwrecked on its shores after setting their sails away from You-Land. Perhaps they merely drift into I-Land, but the result is the same: loneliness and slow death for people who never experience the thrill of *learning to live*.

FIRST STEPS

Learning to live begins with developing positive attitudes and your inner vision.

First, you must be learning to say something positive to everybody all the time.

You say that's not possible. I didn't say you had to *do* it; I said *be learning* to do it. You'll never arrive, but you can be *"on the grow."*

Perhaps as much as ninety-nine percent of our conversation is negative. Some people can't wait for their mouths to open and expose another negative nugget for all to admire. I'm not talking about tongue - in - cheek flattery or snide gilding of the lily, but downright pessimism. I'm convinced that there is nothing that will brighten the atmosphere of a business, church or home like an enthusiastic person who offers a few positive words to others. I believe it is possible to say something positive to everybody about everything all the time *if we want to*.

Did you hear about the two fellows in jail? Tom said to Joe, "Where are you going?" "To the electric chair," Joe replied. "More power to ya," Tom chirped.

That's a little extreme, but Tom's heart was in

the right place. Consider the different effects of the statements: "This rain ruins everything!" and "Look at that beautiful rainbow!" If you'll cultivate the habit of saying something positive to everybody, you won't have to say something to everyone; your image will promote a positive atmosphere wherever you go. But if you aren't working on this, you are drifting near the rocks on the I-Land.

Once a cranky grandpa lay down to take a nap. To have a little fun, his grandson put some Limburger cheese on his mustache. Grandpa awoke with a snort and charged out of the bedroom saying, "This room stinks." And through the house he went. He finally was forced outside only to find out that "The whole world stinks!" This dismal experience can't happen to the person who is learning to say a positive word to everyone.

Second, be learning to see something positive in everything that happens.

Did you ever notice how quickly our minds jump to negative conclusions about things we see and hear? For example, suppose someone called you to the phone and announced, "It's your boss." Is your first thought: "Tremendous, he wants to give me a raise"? No, most of us would react: "Now what did I do?" or, "Who told him?"

I believe that one of the most important habits for us to cultivate is to find something positive in

everything that happens. You may think it's foolish to look for something that isn't there. You're right on that score, but I'm urging you to cultivate being a positive realist and see the positive thing that is already there.

Did you hear about the two positive thinkers in the Army guardhouse? One said to the other, "How long are you in for?" "Thirty days." "What did you do?" "I was AWOL — what are you in for?" "Three days." "What did you do?" "I murdered the General." "How come I got thirty days for being AWOL and you got only three days for murdering the General?" "They're hanging me on Wednesday."

You see, if a man really wants to find something positive in any situation, he can. The problem with most of us is we don't want to. The best things in life don't come easy; they come free, but not easy. Developing this attitude is worth all your effort.

Third, you must be learning to See It Big and Keep It Simple.

We call it SIB-KIS in our office. I've never promoted a universal success formula because I've been learning none of them will work for you unless *you work* for them. My formula won't necessarily work for you, but when you make it yours, it may.

Years ago our office adopted the "SIB-KIS" formula and put it on every bulletin, burned it into every heart and made it a way of life. SIB-KIS stands for: *See It Big — Keep It Simple.*

A fellow says, "What's so important about that?" I'll tell you why it's important to me — it's the opposite of my nature. My nature is to see something small and then complicate it so I can't do anything about it. I need to constantly remind myself that although I can get help from many sources I'm on my own in this area. No one can See It Big and Keep It Simple for me.

It's tremendous to be learning that no matter how big you see things or how simple you keep them you'll never reach the ultimate. No man has ever seen things as big as they could have been seen or kept them as simple as they might be. Sometimes we do well in one area at the expense of the other — like the little boy on the corner with his flop-eared pup.

A new idea is delicate. It can be killed by a sneer or a yawn; it can be stabbed to death by a quip and worried to death by a frown on the right man's brow.
—*Charles Brower*

A salesman passed the corner each day, and after a week he began to pity the boy who was striving to sell his puppy. The salesman knew the boy didn't See It Big. He stopped and said, "Son, do you really want to sell this dog?" The boy replied, "I certainly do."

"Well, you're never going to sell him until you learn to See It Big. What I mean is, take this dog home, clean him up, doll him up, raise your price, make people think they're getting something big, and you'll sell him."

That noon the salesman came by and there was the boy with a puppy that was groomed, perfumed, and beribboned alongside a big sign: TREEEMENNDOUS Puppy For Sale—$5,000."

The salesman gulped and realized he had forgotten to tell the boy about Keeping It Simple. That evening he stopped by to tell the boy the other half of the formula, only to discover that the boy was gone, the puppy was gone and the sign lay there with "SOLD" written across it in big letters.

The salesman couldn't believe it. This kid couldn't have sold the dog for $5,000. His curiosity got the best of him and he rang the boy's doorbell. The boy came to the door and the salesman blurted, "Son, you didn't really sell that dog for $5,000 now, did you?" The boy replied, "Yes, sir, I did and I want to thank you for all your help."

The salesman said, "How in the world did you do it?"

The boy replied, "Oh, it was easy. I just took two $2,500 cats in exchange!"

Watch out that *you* don't get in trouble by See-ing It Big without Keeping It Simple or perhaps Keeping It Simple without Seeing It Big. But, if you'll be learning to see it a little bigger and keep it a little simpler, you're in for some tremendous experiences.

Remember, there is not a school or person in the world that can teach you this. It has to come from your own heart, and you're learning the process right now in what you are doing. You are disciplining yourself to See It a little Bigger and Keep It a little Simpler, or else the other things you're learning will be in vain because you have no way to use your new skill or increased capac-ity.

If you're learning to say something positive to everybody about everything all the time, if you're disciplining your mind to see something positive in everything that happens, and if you're learning to See It Big and Keep It Simple, you have a foundation on which to build a steady, expanding life.

This doesn't mean that everything's going to get easier. Just the opposite. We know that when a person begins to grow, the obstacles get bigger and better. But there's excitement and progress in struggle — and life gets easier only when you're coasting downhill.

WHY — NOT HOW

Did you ever notice the number of people who spend their time learning How To Do It? And after they learn, they accomplish very little before they're looking for a new How To Do It. As soon as they master that, someone announces another How To Do It. Although technical competence in any field is a necessity, the key to using know-how is *know-why*.

The great organizations of the country and the great lives in history have been built on the answers to "why?" You can teach someone how to do a task, but that doesn't assure his doing it.

But let him discover *why* and he'll learn *how* in spite of all obstacles. The key is not how to live but *why you are living*. This stimulus will keep you growing.

Why are you reading this book? I trust it is with a

positive expectation to find answers for living and leading. The answers will come from your own brain-computer as I whirl some of the why-knobs.

Why do some people merely *exist* rather than live the tremendous life? I can't speak for all who are enduring their living-death, but I think many people have simply never been sold on the tremendous life.

At the beginning I mentioned that everybody has been led for better or worse in everything he does all his life. Unless a person in any walk of life becomes a "salesman" of his beliefs and actions, he will never learn much about living, because living is involvement with reality, and the deepest reality is people. We are leading others all the time, unconsciously or deliberately, through our action or their recollection, in one direction or another. We are "selling" our values whenever we're with other people — child, adult, customer, salesman. Our problem is that we often don't realize what we are doing or why. All persons with right motives want to do more than exist — they want to contribute, to have a sense of importance, to be accepted by others. These goals and many others are best accomplished through the tremendous learning-to-live process.

Always dream and shoot higher than you know you can reach. Don't bother just to be better than your contemporaries and predecessors; try to be better than yourself.
— Unknown

2

Seven Laws
of Leadership

God has built certain laws into his universe, and
these laws are no respecter of persons. Too often
wrongly motivated people harness the right laws
for the wrong purposes, while rightly motivated
people assume that sincerity and diligence are
sufficient for success. The latter doesn't get the
right results for the right purposes because they
aren't harnessing the right laws. So I want to dis-
cuss seven laws that are absolutes; following them
will assure you a tremendous adventure in life.
Either you use them and find them working *for*
you, or you will ignore them and find them working *against* you.

THE FIRST LAW OF LEADERSHIP:

Learning To Get Excited About Your Work

This is a law that can't fail. It's a law that stands up. Now, this is a lot different than saying: The first law of leadership is work. Once in a while you hear a guy saying, "Show me a man who will work, and I will show you a success." And I say, "You show me a man who will say that, and I will show you an idiot." Work in itself will not do it. I know; I almost worked myself out of existence a dozen times.

Why do some people work and work and work and never have anything to show for it? And yet some people don't seem to work and they have great results. The First Law of Leadership is not *work* as we usually think of it — though it takes work — but *learning to get excited about your work!*

But a guy says, "Jones, don't you know it's easy to be excited about something glamorous like you're doing or what an executive does? If you had this lousy job of mine you wouldn't talk like that."

I'll let you in on a secret. "Work," wherever you find it, implies only one kind of thing: detail, monotony, preparation, striving, weariness. That's what we all have to overcome, no matter what our work is.

Sure, it's easy to get excited about something I'm not doing. But if I have to do it, and have

to learn and grow and plan and persevere — then work isn't much fun. But the First Law of Leadership is learning to get excited about *my* work, not someone else's. Not the work I'm going to do someday. The First Law of Leadership tells me to get excited about the miserable job I have right now! And, you know, if I can get excited about it while it's miserable, it's going to be tremendous if it ever gets pleasant!

A young man came into my office after graduating number two in his class at an Ivy League school. He said, "Mr. Jones, I've heard about you. I've been interviewed by this company and that company and none of them hit me. I thought you could help me find what I would like to do."

"Oh, one of those poor fellows!" I thought. "I'll give him a little shock treatment." I replied, "You'd like *me* to help *you* find what you'd like to do? How can I help you find what you'd like to do when I haven't been able to find what I would like to do?"

He said, "Don't you like what you're doing?" I bellowed: "I *hate* it! They don't pay very much money to do the things I like to do!"

Do you know what I like? I like to relax; I

like to *talk* about work. I like vacations, conventions, commissions, salary increases, long luncheons. What do I get? Headaches, heartbreaks, turndowns!

But you know what I've been learning? If I don't get excited about what I don't like to do, I don't get much that I do like to be excited about.

I've been learning that life is not doing what you like to do. Real life is doing what you *ought* to do. I've been learning that people who do what they like to do eventually discover that what they thought they like to do, they don't like to do, but people who are learning to do what they don't like to do but ought to do, eventually discover that what they thought they didn't like to do they do like to do.

I earned $10,000 a year when I was 25 years old doing things I didn't like to do. They paid me $25,000 a year when I was 30 to do things I didn't like. When I was 35 they paid me $50,000 a year to do things I didn't like to do.

We don't consider manual work as a curse, or a bitter necessity, not even as a means of making a living. We consider it as a high human function, as a basis of human life, the most dignified thing in the life of the human being, and which ought to be free, creative. Men ought to be proud of it.
— David Ben-Gurion

The salary didn't make those jobs worthwhile — but my efforts and the results were important and worthwhile. Life isn't mainly a matter of doing what you like to do, it's doing what you ought to do and need to do!

I'm glad I was born in time to get in on the old thing called the Depression. There was one thing that everyone was learning in those days without taking any course in psychology: the most exciting thing in the world was to be able to work! To have a job, any kind of a job, was a privilege!

Today everybody's looking for the right kind of job. Sometimes a guy says, "I'm trying to find a job that fits me." I say, "I hope you get something better than that!" We need to be learning that God never made the job that could make a man, but any man who can get excited about his work can make a job.

If you watch a guy who's moving up, you'll see one who knows that he deserves nothing and owes everything. But when he gets to the place that he decides he owes nothing and deserves everything, he will be on his way down before he knows what happened. You watch for it, and see if it is true.

Why is enthusiasm for work so important to success? Let me tell you about a guy who dreamed he inherited a million dollars. He dreamed he went to take a shower that morning and the shower wouldn't shower. He started to shave and the shaver wouldn't shave. He went to get some coffee and the coffee wouldn't perk, and the toaster wouldn't toast. He went out to get the newspaper but the newspaper wasn't there. He went to catch the bus and the bus didn't come. He waited forty-five minutes and finally a guy came puffing down the street. "What's going on around here?" he asked, and the guy gasped, "Haven't you heard? Everybody's inherited a million dollars! Nobody's working any more!"

Just then the man woke up. And he went and had a tremendous shower and a tremendous shave and a tremendous cup of coffee and a tremendous piece of toast. He read a tremendous newspaper and caught a tremendous bus to a tremendous job! What a difference it makes when we are learning to get excited about the work we have today!

A lot of people think enthusiasm or a cheerful spirit is something that *falls* on you! I want to tell you this with all my heart: the most challenging thing you'll ever face in your life is learning every day to be excited about what you're doing.

Sometimes a person says, "I'm preparing for my next job." You had better get excited about the one you've got, or there may not be a next one! Are you excited about what you're doing? This takes *work*. The work in life is learning to be excited about work. Once a person begins to learn a little about it, he's on his way.

There is nothing that can make you more excited about your work than a sense of its importance and urgency. *I believe that the fires of inspiration and greatness in our hearts can be kept burning only by developing this sense of urgency and importance in our work* — not the work I'm going to do, not the work I wish I could do, but the work I am doing now.

A sense of urgency in your work informs you that yesterday is gone forever and tomorrow may never come, but today is in your hands. It lets you know that shirking today's work will add to tomorrow's burden; it helps you accomplish the tasks that today sets before you.

Thank God for the sense of urgency that can change a dull, menial job into a sparkling career. A sense of urgency is not the complete solution, but it is a tremendous step in the right direction. If you don't have a sense of urgency about your work, ask God to give it to you, whatever your work is. Believe that he will and then act accordingly. Rather than wandering through life looking for something that never existed, get excited about your work now and begin to live!

Business is really more agreeable than pleasure; it interests the whole mind, the aggregate nature of man more continuously, and more deeply. But it does not look as if it did. — *Walter Bagehot*

THE SECOND LAW OF LEADERSHIP:

Use or Lose

God gives everyone certain attributes, character-
istics, talents, and then he says, "If you use what
you have, I'll increase it, but if you don't use it,
you'll lose it." Use it or lose it! It's a *law*.

One night when I came out of a seminar a fellow confronted me and said, "Charlie, do you
think it's possible for a person to be excited
about his work, be thrilled and successful and,
three years later, be sick and sorry he ever heard of
the whole lousy mess?"

Oh, oh . . . another person who didn't know
the law of "Use or Lose." You see, one day he
was enjoying and using the talent he had. As a
result he was on the grow and happy. Then he
began to coast, not using what he had, and he
was losing it. One morning he woke up to discover
he had failed. The people who lose what they
had usually blame it on someone else. Consider
this: No one is a failure until he blames somebody else. As long as you accept the blame for
failure, *you* won't be a failure because you're in
a position to change the situation!

Did you hear about the sophisticated burglars
that are operating around the world? One evening they robbed a shoe store. They carefully
took all the shoes out of the boxes and neatly re-
placed the empty boxes on the shelves. Finally
they finished and left the store just as they had

found it — except there were no shoes in the boxes!

The next morning the manager arrived, his usual cheerful self, and held a quick sales meeting with the employees. Then the first customer appeared and he sent out his star salesman: "Go get her, Bill."

Bill rushed over. "Good morning, ma'am," he said. "Put your little footsie right up here. My, what a nice foot! We've got a number from Paris for you that'll knock your eye out. This is . . . excuse me, ma'am, something wrong here. Ma'am, that was the wrong shoe. I want to show you a shoe that's designed for a heavenly foot like . . . oops, that's not it, either. I was saving a pair for my wife that will really get you. Look at this, ma'am . . . uh, one minute, ma'am. I'll be right back.

"Boss, we've got troubles."

"What do you mean, troubles?"

"Boss, we don't have any shoes."

"What do you mean we don't have shoes? Look at all those boxes."

"Boss, all those boxes are empty!"

Yes, sir. That store had been robbed, and the poor owner hadn't even known it! And so it is with millions of people who have been robbed because they didn't practice the law of *Use or Lose*.

Let's take a little inventory of our character stock. A lot of people are not learning the law of *Use or Lose*. This law says that if you're not using what you have, you're losing it. If you're using what you have, you're getting more of it.

Some guy says, "How come I'm twice as smart as he is and he's making twice as much as I am?" I'll tell you why. He is learning to use what he has and get more of it.

Let's check some of the boxes on your shelf. How's your *Total Commitment*? Have you checked it lately? If you have some and you've been using it, you're getting more. If you have some and are not using it, you're losing it.

I tell young men, "If you're ever asked to take on a sideline — something more than what you've put your hand to — demand a fortune for it!" Because if you give up the small amount of total commitment you have, you're bankrupt. A sideline is a slide-line; whatever your hand finds to do, do it with all your might. If you use your total commitment, you'll get more, and more total commitment will get things you really want.

All right, let's check your *Sincerity*. You say, "Oh, boy, am I glad you touched on that because that's my strength."

I don't mean the kind of sincerity you turn on to get your own way. We all know how to act sincere. I'm talking about honest-to-God, genuine sincerity. I'm talking about the kind that grows if you have some and use it, but disappears if you have some and don't use it.

Last year I spoke at a national convention of a company in Hollywood Beach and then went to see my dad in Pompano Beach. I had just enough time to drive up, tell him I love him and give him a little hug and then rush away. There wasn't time for lunch and I was starving when I saw I had to get gas. I thought, "I'll kill two birds with one stone; I'll get gas and run over to the grocery store to get an ice cream sandwich."

I pulled into the gas station and stopped behind another car. As I jumped out, credit card in hand, a fellow came meandering over to my car. I hurriedly said, "Here, take this card and fill my tank. I'll be back in a minute." He replied, "What do you want to do, confuse me?"

My hunger pangs leaped out and snapped: "Take this card and fill this tank or I'll get my gas somewhere else."

I went across the road to get my ice cream sandwich. About half-way across the road, I was hit by a thundering thought: I had just lost a little of my sincerity, and I don't have enough to afford losing any. I could hardly wait to get back

---

A man is relieved and gay when he has put his heart into his work and done his best; but what he has said or done otherwise shall give him no peace.

— Ralph Waldo Emerson

across the street and tell this fellow that I was sorry. When I got back, I said, "Partner, I was rude to you a minute ago and I want to apologize. I'm sorry." You know what he said? "That's all right. *Everybody's rude to me!*"

Yes, we live in a world where many people thrive on being rude to each other. We know how to act sincere, but we don't know much about being sincere, do we? One of the greatest things in the world is to be learning to be a plain, common horse-sense, sincere human being. If more of us could be learning that a little better, maybe our kids would be imitating us rather than devastating us.

It's so easy to spot a con man. I can tell one a mile away — takes one to know one, you know! I've discovered that some of the things I resent about others are reflections of my own faults — and I've been more tolerant since then!

One of the greatest things in the world is for a person who has some sincerity to be using it all the time, with the neighbors, the family, elevator operators, waitresses, *all the time*. If you're not using that little bit of sincerity you have, you're losing it. You can't counterfeit or manufacture real sincerity. And what a thrilling thing it is to meet somebody who's real and plain and genuinely sincere. It's just tremendous!

Let's check the *Loyalty* box. A guy says, "Oh, I'm good on that, too." Yeah, I know what you mean. A lot of people think loyalty is something you give because of what somebody gave you.

That's not loyalty. Loyalty is something you give regardless of what you get back, and in giving loyalty you're getting more loyalty. And out of loyalty flow other great qualities.

Some say, "It'll cost you a lot to be loyal to a family or a company" — but consider what it will cost you if you don't use your loyalty.

How would you like to belong to something where nobody would lay down their lives for what they believed? You can't change the world, but you can change yourself by using what you have and getting a little more of it. I don't know any way to get loyalty except by using and expanding it.

How's your *Discipline*? There's hardly a thing I hate more than discipline. I've always hated it. I remember that disciplinary dad of mine. Almost every morning he'd say, "Son, this hurts me more than it hurts you." I'd say, "Dad, if it hurts you so much, how come you're always doing it?" I hated discipline.

Without loyalty nothing can be accomplished in any sphere. The person who renders loyal service in a humble capacity will be chosen for higher responsibilities, just as the biblical servant who multiplied the one pound given him by his master was made ruler over ten cities, whereas the servant who did not put his pound to use lost that which he had. —B. C. Forbes

But later in life I learned — excuse me, I *began learning* — that one of the greatest attributes a fellow can cultivate and multiply is this thing called discipline. Discipline is a quality. You start with a little bit of it, you submit yourself to authority and a job and a goal and you learn a bit more about discipline.

The person who is not learning about discipline by subjecting himself to authority can try all the self-disciplining he wants, but he'll never be successful! He has no discipline to apply discipline. Many people fail because they refuse to exercise this essential quality. Even in discouragement and defeat, discipline will spur you to keep constructively busy while you leave behind doubt, worry and self-pity.

Some of us have the spirit: "I'll do anything except . . ." Don't ever say that! If you do, that's the very thing you have to do to begin to learn this quality that you need as much as any other thing — discipline.

I hope you haven't let that sophisticated burglar clean you out of your stock-in-traits when you weren't watching. Remember, he's working on you and me all the time. There's simply no other way to get more of what you need than by using what you have.

THE THIRD LAW OF LEADERSHIP:

Production to Perfection

Once in a while I meet a man who says, "You

know, I don't believe in going off half-cocked. When I do something, it's got to be perfect."

I don't know if you heard about Sam's clothing store, but Sam was quite a guy. He knew about the law of production to perfection. One day John came in to see Sam. He says, "Sam, I want to buy a suit."

Sam says, "S-h-h!"
He said, "What d'ya mean, S-h-h?"
"We don't sell suits here."
John said, "Wh-wh-what are all these things?"
Sam said, "Well, uh, when you come in here to buy a suit, it's not — here, walk over this way — it's not as if we could sell you one off the rack. When you come in here to buy a suit, it's a project! We make it an affair. We've got to know the real you. We've got to know your attitude and your aptitude, your likes and your dislikes. And when we get to know the real you, we pick the right wool that fits you. We even go to England to pick the right sheep that fits you. And the silk lining — we go to Japan to get the right silk; we even pick out the right worm! And the buttons; we go to Alaska to pick the elk that fits you."

John interrupts: "Wait a minute, Sam. I've got to have a suit today!"

Sam purrs: "You'll have it!"

Now, I believe in doing things right. In fact, one of my frequent prayers, the cry of my heart, is "O God, let me do one thing right before I die." But I add, "In the meantime, Lord, help me do *something!*"

There's a law that says if you're not learning to make something happen today you won't know much about perfection tomorrow. As a young salesman, I was learning this every step of the way. As a husband, father, Sunday school teacher — you name it — my heart delighted in doing *something,* because while it might have been better had I waited a little longer, many of those somethings might not have been done at all.

If you major in perfection, you'll produce little more than dreams. But *production* will teach you a little about perfection in daily living.

He that leaveth nothing to chance will do few things ill, but he will do very few things.
— *Charles Baudelaire*

You will never stub your toe standing still. The faster you go, the more chance there is of stubbing your toe, but the more chance you have of getting somewhere.
— *Charles F. Kettering*

THE FOURTH LAW OF LEADERSHIP:

Give to Get

"I really believe that law," someone says. "My grandad taught me that. And my wife, she says that too. And just last week the pastor preached on it. He said, 'If you give, you'll get!' "

Don't you believe it! It's not true!

You've heard of the guy who says, "Well, my secret of success is: I gave. Yes, I gave and gave and gave and gave," ("and look at all I got," says his manner).

People who give to get would be better off if they didn't get anything. I know people who have been ruined by what they got because they

didn't get what they thought they were going to get — *it got them,* and there's a difference!

This is not only a play on words. There *is* a healthy "giving to get," but it is far different from what we usually mean.

Leadership is learning to give whether you get anything or not! If you ever give something to get something, *you're not giving* in the true sense of the word, *you're trading!*

Actually, we don't know much about giving.

Do you realize one of the great problems in marriage is that we know so little about giving? We know all about trading, but not giving.

If a person is *learning to give whether he gets anything or not,* he is really giving. And if you'll give — whether you get anything or not — you always get a greater capacity to give. This increasing capacity forms a ready reservoir for a marketable commodity which will always enable you to produce and give, to live confidently and securely, in a world that's running scared to death (no matter what the bank account says).

You may lose your reputation, your home and even your family, but you can't lose your capacity to give *if you're learning to give.* But *you're not really giving* if you give to get something other than a greater capacity to give.

Once a fellow said to me, "You know why I can't work six days a week, twenty hours a day?" "Why?" I asked. "Because this isn't my business. If this were my own business, boy, I could put out! But I have no proprietary interest here. If it were something I could leave to my kids, I'd work night and day. I'd . . ."

Wait a minute. I worked sixteen years for a company where I drew a paycheck. In those six-

---

No person was ever honored for what he received. Honor has been the reward for what he gave. — *Calvin Coolidge*

teen years I didn't work one time for that company. Whom was I working for? I was working for Charles E. Jones and his six little bread-snappers! And there were a lot of times when I knew I was giving and I wasn't getting anything except heartaches and misery, and problems on problems. But I was aware I was learning to give, in the true sense.

The young contractor who married a contractor's daughter had to learn the hard way. The father-in-law wanted to give a boost to his new son-in-law.

"Son," he said, "I don't want you to start at the bottom where I did. So I want you to go out and build the most tremendous house this town has ever seen, put the best of everything in it, make it a palace, and turn it over to me."

Well, this was an opportunity to make a killing. He hurried out to slap together a building that would survive two fairly stiff gales. In short order he was back to dear old dad. "Well, Dad, it's finished."

"Is it tremendous, is it a palace like I asked?"

"Yes-siree, Dad."

"Is it really the finest house ever built, son?"

"Yes-siree, Dad."

"All right, where is the bill? Is there a good profit in it for you?"

"Yes-siree, Dad."

"Very good. Here is your check, and where is the deed?"

As he looked at the deed, the father said, "I

didn't tell you why I wanted that house to be the best house ever built. I wanted to do something special for you and my daughter to show you how much I love you . . . here, take the deed, go live in the house — you built it for yourself!"

The young gold-bricker crept out a shattered, frustrated man. He thought he was making a fortune at his father's expense by saving money on inferior materials and short-cuts, but he cheated only himself.

Contractor or not, you're building a life. A better life rises from an increasing capacity to give. Real giving makes real living, creating a capacity to give something that no one else can.

I want to assure you that the person hasn't lived who practiced this law to its full potential. There's not a man, including myself, who knows very much about giving. But by the grace of God anyone can be doing a better job of learning the law of *Give to Get*. And remember, what you get is not a return gift but a greater capacity to go beyond where you are. That's a law for growing!

THE FIFTH LAW OF LEADERSHIP:

Exposure to Experience

In the beginning of life, God gives every person a psychological key ring. And he gives a law that says, "Every time you expose yourself to another situation, I'll give you another key of experience for your key ring."

Soon the key ring begins to be filled with experiences, and then we begin to know how to pick the right key to unlock the situation we face. The person who's not learning the law of *Exposure to Experience* is fumbling around trying to find a key that he doesn't have, or he has it somewhere and wastes times trying to find it because he hasn't been using it. Then, when he gets to the key, somebody else has come along and taken home the bacon.

Sometimes the fellow who gets lots of bacon decides to relax and enjoy it. He gets to be 40 or 45, and his income has spiraled up steadily. "It's about time I started tapering off," he tells himself. The income keeps rising, and the living success story says: "It's about time I started enjoying my reward."

Trouble!

What makes a person really produce? It's knowing that he owes a lot and deserves little. But when a person reaches the place where he thinks, "I owe little and I deserve a lot," he's heading downhill.

One of the biggest lies ever palmed off on man is: "Success is a reward to be enjoyed." I don't know one person who is using his success as a reward and is genuinely happy. We're told: "To whom much is given, of him shall much be required." Success is not a reward to be enjoyed but a trust to be administered.

I know people around the country who could go fishing for the rest of their lives but they prefer to be dynamically active and they're having the time of their lives.

This is an exciting law because its practice makes things get better and better with added years. As you accumulate experiences you use those keys over and over again. Eventually you know which keys unlock the doors, and you slip through while the inexperienced people search feverishly to see if they have a key. The oldtimer who is learning the law of *Exposure to Experience* doesn't need the stamina that he once needed; he knows how to get to the heart of a problem and prescribe a remedy.

The most dynamic, tremendous people who have made an impact on my life have been over 60 years old. Some are over 70, and last year the man whose life excited me the most was over 80!

Most people who are getting old waste time wishing they were young again. I don't wish I were young again — I had plenty of fun, but the young are miserable with unanswered questions — at least I was. Look at some of these dynamic old geezers; this sort of exuberance could ruin the Senior Citizen program! I'm convinced that practicing this law can make every year of your life more tremendous than the last.

It's a shame that people *get old* rather than *grow old*. A person who gets old is not practicing the law of *Exposure to Experience*. Getting old means you're drifting, not growing. And that means getting shallow, and cynical, and thankless. But if you grow old, you're getting deeper and richer and fuller. It's exciting to grow old as you practice the law of *Exposure to Experience*.

Now, there's no way to learn this law of experience other than through exposure. I didn't get much business in my early days, but I sure got a lot of exposure, and that exposure gave me a lot of experience that eventually got me a lot of business.

It's a law that absolutely has no short-cuts. You have to take the main route through all the traffic, but it gets you where you want to go.

SIXTH LAW OF LEADERSHIP:

Flexible Planning

This is the age of the planner, the organizer. You go to a seminar and hear some dynamic lecturer say: "Show me a man who plans, and I'll show you a success." I say (to myself, of course), "Show me a man who'll say that and I'll show you an idiot."

Statistics are no substitute for judgment.
— *Henry Clay*

Don't ever think that planning will do it. I used to plan plans to end all plans, and I almost planned myself out of business a half-dozen times. Planning can't be the answer!

You've heard the sad sack who moans, "I'm no quitter. I've tried six plans, but I'm not quitting yet. I'm making one more plan. If this plan doesn't work, I've had it." I've got news for him. He's had it already!

Now, I believe in planning, but the key is not "planning," it's *Flexible Planning*. Have a plan — a flexible one.

Do you know what Flexible Planning means? It means: *whatever can go wrong . . . will go wrong!* That's right! And since we know that whatever can go wrong may go wrong at the wrong time, *Flexible Planning* says: plan on your plan going wrong so that you're ready with an alternate plan because *"That's my plan!"*

Do you know that a lot of people are miserable because they expect everything to go right? They're *asking* for misery! I expect things to go wrong, and so I'm jubilant all the time! A smart guy asked me: "What if something goes right?" Easy; I can work it in. I haven't had much trouble with that yet!

It may serve as a comfort to us, in all our calamities and afflictions, that he that lost anything and gets wisdom by it is a gainer by the loss. —*Sir Roger L'Estrange*

Try this tomorrow morning when you start out. Say, "Lord, send me some miserable problems today." I've done it, and no sooner did I get started than I said, "You sure answered that prayer in a hurry." You may say you don't have to pray such a prayer — the miserable problems come anyway. But you aren't prepared for them, are you?

I remember when I came into the business I was told about the product and given sales training. I could hardly wait to get out in the field. Finally the big day came and I asked the manager, "Whom do I sell?" He said, "The world is your market!" The whole world, wow!

But I was disorganized. I was like that Texan who rushed into the airport and demanded: "Gimme a ticket!" "Where to?" asked the agent, fumbling with the tickets. "It doesn't matter — I've got business *all over*," trumpeted the Texan.

Talk about confusion! I was the master of it. I used to jump in my car before I completely fell apart and race to the manager's office. I'd rush in and say, "I've got a problem." And he'd say, "Let me tell you what it is; your problem is planning." I thought, "Oh, is he smart! I didn't even

tell him the problem and he gave me the answer!"
That was pretty good until the twentieth time;
then I realized it was a canned sales talk. You
know the trouble with canned sales talks? The
customers don't know their parts!

We need to be learning *Flexible Planning*. The
mark of a man who is growing is his understand-
ing that things go wrong to make us more right.
God never breaks a man down with problems except to build him up.

The wild stallion may look beautiful on the
mesa with his mane blowing in the wind, but he
isn't much use until somebody breaks him so he
can pull a load or carry a rider. Neither is a person much good until he is harnessed to team-
work and disciplined to guidance. God trains a
man so the man can run free. That's an old law;
you can fight it, but you'll never change it.

Imagine how superficial our lives would be if
God didn't send circumstances that seem disas-
trous for the moment but later prove enriching
and meaningful.

One of my employees told me, "I'm going to
have to quit." I asked him why. "Well, I don't
think this is God's will for me. Things are awful."
"They're awful?" I said. "That means you're
right where you ought to be! This can make you
a success!"

I'll never forget the big case I sold after I'd
been in the business three years. Whoooo, was I
licking my chops! We built a big, beautiful home
on the profits. But sometimes things get confused

in pension cases, and this one was the confusion of all confusions. Finally I had to give all my earnings back, and I was stuck with that fancy home.

That's always been the way with me. So I've been learning that while I can't determine in life when I'm going to get kicked, I can determine which way I'm going to go when I get kicked.

I guess there's no way to grow up without some going down. No humility without humiliations. A person becomes terribly frustrated and bitter if he ignores the law of *Flexible Planning*.

I heard about a boy who went to work in a grocery store after graduating from high school, and a couple of weeks later his dad said, "Son, let's now talk about college."

"Oh, Dad, I didn't tell you. I'm not going to college."

"You're not going to college? Why?"

"I'm not going to college because I found my life's work."

"What do you mean — you found your life's work?"

"You know," he said, "I'm driving the truck there, and I love driving the truck delivering groceries. The boss is happy; I just got a raise! It's really wonderful work."

"Well, son, you can do something besides drive a truck and deliver groceries all your life."

But the boy said, "Wait a minute. Didn't you tell me life is to be happy?"

"Yes."

"Well, I'm happy, and that's what I'm going to do. I'm not going to college!"

Well, the dad was the victim of his own myopia. Life isn't to be happy; it is to be *growing*. The dad realized he had to take another approach. There was no use telling a sixteen-year-old the answers because he knew all the answers! So Dad went down to the grocery and said, "John, you're going to have to fire my son."

"What do you mean, fire your son? I've never known a boy like this. He's the most wonderful boy I've ever seen. I just gave him a raise. Shines that truck; keeps people happy. Boy, it's great."

"Well, he's not going to college," said the father, "and if you don't fire him you're going to ruin his life."

The grocer realized he had to do something. On Friday the kid came in to get his pay, and the grocer said, "Just a minute!" And the kid says, "Yes?" He said, "You're fired."

"What'd I do?"

"You're fired."

"What's wrong?"

Perseverance and tact are the two great qualities most valuable for all men who would mount, but especially for those who have to step out of the crowd.

— Benjamin Disraeli

"You're fired!"

"Wh—"

"You're fired!"

The kid got the idea he was fired. He went home, all dejected. He said, "All right, Dad. I'll go to school."

This is a true story. Some thirty years later, after the boy had gone on to become president of one of the leading universities, he said to his dad, "I want to thank you for the time you got me fired."

Now, it's a hard lesson to be learning, but the law of *Flexible Planning* says to capitalize on your heartbreaks and misery or you'll miss the best in life. Make the things that go wrong a part of your plan, and you will be far ahead of where you were when you were waiting for something to happen your way.

This doesn't mean you shouldn't plan. Charles Schwab, then president of Bethlehem Steel, granted an interview to Ivy Lee, an extraordinary management consultant. Lee told Schwab that his consulting firm could uncover opportunities for improvement of the company's operations. Schwab said he already knew of more things that should be done than he and his staff could get to. What was needed was "not more knowing, but more going."

"If you can show us a way to get more things done," Schwab said, "I'll be glad to listen to you. And, if it works, I'll pay you whatever you ask within reason."

Lee answered, "If that is what you want, I will show you a method that will increase your personal management efficiency, and that of anyone else who applies it, by at least fifty percent."

He handed Schwab a blank piece of paper and said, "Write down the most important things you have to do tomorrow." Schwab did as requested; it took about five minutes.

Lee then said, "Now, number them in the order of their true importance." This took a little longer because Schwab wanted to be sure of what he was doing.

Finally Lee instructed, "The first thing tomorrow morning, start working on item Number 1, and stay with it until it is completed. Then take item Number 2 the same way. Then Number 3, and so on. Don't worry if you don't complete everything on the schedule. At least you will have completed the most important projects before getting to the less important ones. If you can't finish all that you planned for tomorrow with this system, there's no other way you would have finished. And without this system you probably would have taken much longer to complete what you set out to do, without taking care of things in the order of their real value to you and your company.

"Do this every working day," Lee went on. "After you have convinced yourself of the value of this system, have your men try it. Try it as long as you like, and then send me your check for whatever you think the idea is worth."

In a few weeks, Charles Schwab sent Ivy Lee a check for $25,000.

Schwab reportedly stated that this lesson was the most profitable one he learned in his business career. It was later said that this was the plan largely responsible for turning a little steel company into one of the largest steel producers in the world. It also helped make Charles Schwab a multi-millionaire.

That's an incredibly simple way to plan your day to get the most out of the available time, though it is not a strategy for accomplishing a goal. You need *Flexible Planning* for that.

Flexible Planning says to have a plan that enables you to roll with the punches, to adapt and adjust. Be learning to capitalize on things that go wrong, making them stepping stones of progress. That makes the "wrong" things "right," an exchange that anyone should appreciate.

SEVENTH LAW OF LEADERSHIP:

Motivated to Motivating

Today we're surrounded by motivators — peo-

Your circumstances may be uncongenial, but they shall not long remain so if you but perceive an ideal and strive to reach it. You cannot travel within and stand still without.
—*James Lane Allen*

ple and things strive to motivate people to buy a product, pay for advice or enlist in a cause. Motivation classes are crammed and motivation books are best-sellers. Motivation is big business!

But look closely at these motivators — some reach the point where they can motivate anybody into doing anything and success is running out their ears, yet they are miserable because they forgot to learn how to motivate themselves!

Which would you rather be — a miserable, successful motivator or a happy, motivated flop? I would rather be a happy, motivated flop. If I am learning to be motivated, I'll eventually become a successful motivator of others, and be happy doing it. The motivator who can motivate everybody but himself may win the world but he'll never enjoy it.

How well I remember my great desire as a young salesman to become a master motivator. I couldn't wait to finish my training so I could use my dynamic motivational skills. The sales presentations were powerful, in fact they were so powerful that I felt I had to temper them or the prospect might die of a heart attack before I asked him to buy. I knew no one could resist the logic, the benefits, the security, the peace of mind — there hardly seemed a problem in the world that my presentation couldn't solve!

I recall how I expected the prospect to snatch the pen from my hand to sign on the dotted line . . . but he never did. Right in the hottest part of the sizzle, my prospect would yawn or

interrupt with some scintillating statement like, "I'm insurance-poor," or "I have $5,000 with double *identity!*"

My heart would hit the floor. I'd sink so low I'd have to reach up to touch bottom. You never saw a more discouraged young salesman than I was. I soon began to be learning my problem wasn't how to motivate people — my problem was how to keep them from demotivating me!

Sometimes I would become so discouraged there was nothing to do but go cry on the boss' shoulder, only to find he was more discouraged than I was! The prospects were discouraging me, the boss was discouraging me, friends were discouraging me, and I thought at times even my wife was discouraging me.

Sometimes a fellow at a seminar will come up and murmur: "Do you know why I'm not a success? I have a miserable wife."

I enjoy giving these fellows the shock treatment: "Do you really have a miserable wife? Well, you don't know how lucky you are. The best asset a man can have is a *miserable wife!* What if my wife had been sympathetic when I went home and told her how miserable things were and she said, 'Oh, my sweet little daddy, you stay home here with mommy and I'll take care of you'? We would have consoled each other amongst our furniture on the sidewalk!"

If you have a miserable wife, you'll keep working or she'll remind you what an idiot you were to take such a job in the first place. But don't despair if you don't have a miserable wife; you can probably make the grade without this asset.

I'm kidding, but I want to make it clear that there are no barriers you can't overcome if you are learning to be motivated. I believe with all my heart that everything that touches your life is to make you a more deeply motivated person — who in turn can motivate others to higher goals.

Some people ask what is my secret of being motivated. Well, I didn't find it — it found me. One of my achievements during my first five years in selling was five years of consecutive weekly production. This means that I never missed one week in selling a policy. This sounds impressive, but it's not the whole truth.

The whole truth is that I believed in goals and so I made a vow that I would sell a policy every week *or buy one*. Let me tell you, after I bought 22 policies I began to get motivated! Little did I realize that a simple vow would have the greatest influence on my work the rest of my life. For out of that vow and what it cost me to keep it, I began to learn *involvement and commitment*.

Some people get involved with their work but

are not committed. Others are committed but don't get deeply involved. The two go together, and I'm convinced that there is no way to learn to be a motivated person without being totally involved and committed to whatever you are engaged in!

The greatest motivations I've had have come from my own heart and home. Someone else's experience or story can never motivate you as deeply as your own.

I used to tell a prospect who said he was insurance-poor that he was actually insurance-rich. But I discovered something far more effective through a little episode at home. This experience allowed me to agree wholeheartedly with an insurance-poor prospect, but gave me additional motivation to pass on to him.

My son Jere, six years old at the time, came in from the yard one day yelling at the top of his lungs for his mother. Naturally, this distracted me from my work in my office (really our living room — we had moved the furniture into the hallway). Jere upped his yell several decibels, and I thought, "I can't wait to get successful so I can move to a plush office downtown where I can fail in style."

Finally Jere gave up, and just then Gloria came up from the basement where she had been running the washer. She said, "What did you want, Jere?" He replied, "Nothing; just wanted to know where you were."

I've told that story thousands of times because

it shows why I pay the premiums on those twenty-two policies. I may never leave my six children an empire, a block of real estate or a huge stock portfolio, but I'm going to leave them a priceless gift: a fulltime mother. Because of my life insurance all six could come yelling for their mother knowing she was somewhere around the house, even though she didn't answer.

Another time I was sitting in the rocker reading the paper when eight-year-old Pam slipped her little blonde head under my arm and wiggled onto my lap. I kept reading and then she said those few words that have helped me sell millions of dollars in life insurance. Looking at me with big, sad eyes, she said, "Daddy, if you won't ever leave me, I won't ever leave you."

I couldn't understand what prompted those words, but I immediately thought: "Well, dearest, I would never leave you, but if the Lord should

No man can fight his way to the top and stay at the top without exercising the fullest measure of grit, courage, determination, resolution. Every man who gets anywhere does so because he has first firmly resolved to progress in the world and then has enough stick-to-it-tiveness to transform his resolution into reality. Without resolution, no man can win any worthwhile place among his fellow men. —B. C. Forbes

rule otherwise at least I'll never leave you *without.*"

Years ago I learned there were two kinds of dads, the *see*-kind and the *have*-kind. The see-kind says, "I want my family to have everything I can give them as long as I'm here to see it." The have-kind says, "I want them to have it whether I'm here to see it or not."

That is what happened to me as a result of commitment and involvement.

You say, "I'm not in the insurance field," or "I don't have a selling career." Listen, the principles we are talking about are the same for a student, wife, office worker, salesman, or whatever you are. The great things in your life will be greater if you are capitalizing on them to help you *be motivated.* Remember, you are building a life, not an empire. One of my best friends got mixed up on this very thing and lost almost everything of value.

I've heard men say, "I put my business first," and other men say, "I put my family first." A few say, "I put my church first." (The truth is they probably put themselves first.) But I've found that my best lessons for business come from my family and church. And the best lessons for my family come from my business and church. And the best lessons for church come from my family and business.

Another son, Jeff, gave me some of the best motivation training of my life. When he was six, I asked Jeff what he wanted to do with his life.

Now get this, six years old, and he still had no idea what he wanted to do with his life!

When I was six, I knew what I wanted to be. One day I wanted to be a fighter pilot, the next day I wanted to be a French Foreign Legionnaire. I wanted to be a boxer. I wanted to be a policeman. I always wanted to be something. Not my Jeff; still drifting.

So I said, "Jeff, we're going to have a little project. Here's a *Boys' Life* — you pick out a job. You're going to do something, partner." The next day he had it all worked out: he was joining the Junior Executive Sales Club of America. He filled out the coupon and sent it in.

I find that kids are dying to get on with the show! They want to do something. They're not getting much direction from anybody — except in the wrong way.

Two weeks later when I came home, Jeff greeted me at the door, "Look, Dad." And here was the biggest box of greeting cards I'd ever seen. I opened it up. There was a badge, credentials, and a notice that said, "Send in the money in 30 days." Jeff said, "What do I do now?" I said, "Well, you have to learn the sales talk first."

Every night I would come home and Jeff would say, "Well, Dad, am I ready?" I'd say, "Have you got the sales talk down?" He'd say, "No." I said, "You're not going out there adlibbing if you're going to represent me. I want you to know what you are going to say."

Two weeks later, Jeff finally told me: "I don't like that sales talk." "Well, write one yourself," I said.

Next morning at the breakfast table, there was a little piece of paper that said, "Good morning, Mrs. Smith, I'm Jeffrey John Jones. I represent the Sales Club of America." That's all! Two weeks had gone by and in two more weeks I had to send in the money! That night I came home and I told Jeff, "Get out the tape recorder; we're going to make up a talk. We're going to work until you have a sales talk."

We started rehearsing; the talk was like this: "Good morning, Mrs. Smith, I'm Jeffrey John Jones of the Junior Executive Sales Club of America. Would you look at these greeting cards, please? You'll notice they carry the Good House-keeping Seal of Approval, and are an exception-ally good value at only $1.25 per box. Would you like one or two boxes (smile) pleeeeze?"

We rehearsed and rehearsed, and as we used the tape recorder to play back, I could see the ti-ger begin to develop in Jeff. Finally he said, "Am I ready yet?" I said, "No, you're not ready yet. You know how it goes here, but you don't know how it is in the field. You go out into the hall, and I'll be your prospect. Take two boxes with you, knock on the door, and I'll show you what to expect when you get out in the field."

Bursting with excitement and confidence, Jeff leaped into the hall to show me his power. He thought he was really ready. He knocked on the door. I threw open the door with a scowl and a roar: "What do you mean busting in on my lunch!" The Junior Executive Salesman sank slowly to the floor in a state of shock.

I got him up and we started over. I let him get through the second line, and I shot him down, the third line and I shot him down. His mother downstairs thought I was killing her baby! But I was getting her baby ready for a little living! You know who's "killing their baby" today? The parent who is raising his kid to think the world is going to give him a hug and a kiss every time he turns around. I was getting this boy of mine ready for reality!

Finally Jeff had his talk down pat and he made it through. "Well," he said, "are we ready?" I said, "You're ready. Here's how we start. Go down St. John's Road with two boxes. Wear a coat and a tie. As soon as you get ten no's, make a beeline for the house." (I knew that more than ten no's would ruin him.) "And as soon as two people say yes, make a beeline for the house." (I knew that more than two yesses might ruin him, too — I've seen prosperity kill about as many salesmen as failure has. He went out and sold those cards like hot cakes!)

Then one day he disobeyed me. On an unbelievably hot July day Jeff came in after taking

---

Work as hard as you can, get as much as you can, give as much as you can.

nineteen straight no's. He was beaten, drenched with perspiration, and he slumped on the sofa. He said, "If they want any cards from me from now on, they'll have to come and get 'em!"

I said, "Now wait a minute, Jeff. You've just had a hard day, pardner." "Oh, Dad," he said, "all the other kids have found out what I'm doing and they're selling cards too."

I said, "I *know* somebody out there wants to buy." (Somebody *had* to be buying; I could never use that many greeting cards.) I said, "You need somebody to go along with you. You've got to get yourself a helper. Take your sister Candy along. Pay her 10¢ to carry the boxes, and she'll give you moral support."

Did they get out there and encourage each other like I thought? No. They got out there and both started griping, and they *both quit!* (That was a good reminder for me: if you get discouraged, don't cry on a friend's shoulder. A friend will give you sympathy, and you're already giving yourself twice as much sympathy as you need. You'd better get back into the swing of things and *work* all the harder.)

Now I had all these cards on my hands, plus two quitters. I had to come up with something. "Jeff, on Saturday I'm going out with you myself." Then I called up one of my assistants and said, "Jack, on Saturday we're coming over to Green Lane Farms, and Jeff's in a slump. If I don't get him out of this slump soon, I'll have to buy these cards myself. I'll let him out two houses from your house. I want him to get two no's and then have a yes waiting at your house."

And so we got over to Green Lane Farms on Saturday. The first house said yes instead of no, and the second house said yes. You should have seen Jeff's face as he ran back to the car with a 1000 percent batting average! He was motivated!

Last year I lent Jeff $24 to finance a home-cleaning product. He took thirty-eight no's on a hot August day, but he didn't quit. He is learning that if you stay motivated you don't mind the no's, and he knows there is a "Green-Lane-Farm" experience ahead if you keep going.

One of the greatest stories I've heard that shows the difference between outward and inward motivation is told by Bob Richards, the former pole-vault champion. A college boy on the football team was a number-one goof-off, a gold-bricker. He liked to hear the cheers, but not to charge the line. He liked to wear the suit, but not to practice. He didn't like to put out.

One day the players were doing fifty laps and this showpiece was doing his usual five. The coach came over and said, "Hey, kid, here's a telegram for you."

The kid says, "Read it for me, coach." He was so lazy he didn't even like to read.

Coach opened it up and read: "Dear son, your father's dead. Come home immediately." The coach swallowed hard. He said, "Take the rest of the week off." He didn't care if he took the rest of the year off.

Well, funny thing, game time came on Friday and here comes the team rushing out on the field, and lo and behold, the last kid out was the goof-off. No sooner did the gun sound than the kid was saying, "Coach, can I play today? Can I play?"

The coach thought, "Kid, you're not playing today. This is homecoming. This is the big game. We need every real guy we have, and you're not one of them."

Everytime the coach turned around, the kid badgered him: "Coach, please let me play. Coach, I've got to play."

The first quarter ended with the score lopsided against ol' alma mater. At half-time the coach braced them in the locker room with a fight talk. "All right, men, get out there and hit 'em. This is a long way from being over. Win this one for the old coacheroo!"

The team rushed out and began tripping over their own feet again. The coach, mumbling to himself, began writing out his resignation. And up came this kid. "Coach, coach, let me play, please!" The coach looked up at the scoreboard. "All right," he said, "get in there, kid. You can't hurt nothin' now."

No sooner did the kid hit the field than his team began to explode. He ran, passed, blocked, tackled like a star. The electricity leaped to the team. The score began to even up. In the closing seconds of the game this kid intercepted a pass and ran all the way for the winning touchdown!

Whooooo! The stands broke loose. Pandemonium. People hoisted the hero onto their shoulders. Such cheering you never heard. Finally the excitement subsided and the coach got over to the kid and said, "I never saw anything like that. What in the world happened to you out there?"

He said, "Coach, you know my dad died last week."

"Yes," he said, "I read you the telegram."

"Well, coach," he said, "my dad was blind. And today was the first day he ever saw me play!"

Wouldn't it be great if life were a game? Wouldn't it be wonderful if the field of life had cheering sections on each side, and when we reached the impossible situation and didn't know how to go on and no one understood us and we're about ready to fold and say those terrible words, "I quit," wouldn't it be wonderful if the stands would come alive and they'd yell, "Charlie, boy, keep on going; we're with you!" I'd say, "Whooooo! That's all I needed." Boy, I'd go on down the field to another touchdown!

But life isn't a game, is it? It's a battlefield.

Know-how is tremendous when you know-why; know-how lets you drive it, knowing-why drives you.
                                    —*C. E. J.*

Instead of players and spectators, we're all soldiers, including some goldbrickers and some AWOLs! But we're all in the struggle, whether we know it or not. And the person who knows how to be motivated doesn't need any cheering section. He has motivation built in. He's not looking for a crutch that might break, a bonus that will be taxed away; he's learning motivation from within. What really makes a man is his inner dynamic and the learning of the law of being motivated, not the power of motivating others. If you are motivated, you will motivate others inevitably. And isn't it exciting to be around people who are motivated? Whooooo!

I hope all of this helps you frame your thoughts with words so you can think through these laws that you've already known instinctively. Our innate notions about these laws are basically correct, but so many things in life seem at war against these laws in an attempt to disprove them. But practice will prove them, and only the people who are exercising these basic laws are moving ahead and growing in leadership — so be learning them!

Truth and love are two of the most powerful things in the world; and when they both go together they cannot easily be withstood.
— Ralph Cudworth

3

Three Decisions in Life

A person can either drive himself or be driven; motivation makes the difference. I believe my motivation has been a steady flow from life's three great decisions. There are only three decisions in life. Someone says, "What do you mean, Charlie? I made about forty-five decisions yesterday."

No, not really. Those weren't basic decisions. There are only three basic decisions in life, and when you make them they shape everything else and they require everything you have to abide by them.

The three great decisions are: 1) Whom are you going to live your life with? 2) What are you going to live your life in? 3) What are you going to live your life for?

WHOM ARE YOU GOING
TO LIVE YOUR LIFE WITH?

I listen to broadcasts at night when I'm relaxing, or I read magazines on the plane and I'm told over and over: "A successful marriage is based upon compatibility." Compatibility! If a successful marriage is based on compatibility, I must be the most miserable married man around!

When my wife and I were courting each other, we were two of the most compatible people that ever lived. We were so compatible it hurt! Before we were married, she just loved to do things *my* way. And then we got married — and I discovered *she* had a way that she liked very much.

Before we were married, she'd look up into my eyes and say, "Oh, my dearest, I understand you so well!" I thought, "Whooooo, I don't even understand myself, and here's somebody who does!" I grabbed her up quick; I married her. And what was the first thing I discovered? She'd lied. It turned out that she *didn't* understand me, and now after twenty years she still says, "You know, the better I get to know you, the less I understand you."

So there we were, married. She fooled me and I fooled her, and we were stuck. Well, I could have traded her in on a new model, but I had an investment here. So I decided to rehabilitate her. The trouble was that she wanted to rehabilitate me.

I always knew I was a mouse, but I never

 told her because I thought if I could marry her she would be what I needed to help me grow and develop my masculinity. That way, I could become a man before she found out she'd married a mouse. Could I help it that she found out the truth too soon?

Well, I didn't get what I thought I was getting, either.

Actually, we each had a plan. She knew I was going to change her and make her better, and I knew she was going to change me and make me better. The plans were working fine at first. I was all set to let her change me and make me better as soon as I finished making her better. But she ruined everything: she wouldn't let me change her until she changed me! I didn't go for that. I decided to die the way I am.

Sure, we *acted* happy, like other couples, but we probably didn't fool many people. We needed to be learning that two people come together to grow old together. The sweetest scene in the world is two people growing old together, growing deeper, richer and fuller in sharing.

You know what growing means? Growing means *growing pains*: it means *changing*. When two people come together and don't let each other change each other, they may wind up *exchanging* each other.

Listen, the secret of a happy marriage is not compatibility, it is integrity, the integrity of the two people to make the marriage decision, make it truly theirs, and die by it. When my wife married me it was for better or worse (mostly worse), richer or poorer (mostly poorer), till death do us part (that settles that).

I got to be called a husband by getting married, but I was married several years before I knew what a husband was. I was married for years before I ever talked to my wife! No, it wasn't a silent marriage — it was very noisy, but we didn't say much of consequence to each other.

I've found there are a lot of men and women who live together and raise a family and never know what it is to really talk to each other. Some people don't even have real talks with their children.

Genuine communication in the family is one of the hardest things in the world to learn. It takes a lot of effort, some training, some growing and some changing. I can point to the spot where I first really talked to my wife.

Love does not make you weak, because it is the source of all strength, but it makes you see the nothingness of the illusory strength on which you depended before you knew it.
— Leon Bloy

I imagine this is hard to believe, but I lectured all across America on confidence and courage to thousands of people while I couldn't get up enough courage to pray with my wife and family. It took three years. I was afraid they'd be embarrassed or think that I was getting too religious. But I knew it was my responsibility to lead the family, and something needed to be done to bring us closer together. I never knew my wife or children well until finally I began to use a little courage to express love and leadership through praying together.

One of the great blessings in my life came one night when my wife and I prayed together. I don't mean we made religious noises; we just talked to God about some things we couldn't seem to say to each other.

I remember I was irritated with her over some little thing, and that's why it hit me so hard. She prayed first that night and said something like this: "Dear God, thank you for this good husband you've given me, forgive me for not being a better wife, help me be better."

As she prayed her words crushed me. I could see very clearly she wasn't at fault. I was the scoundrel. I wasn't the husband I should have been. I wasn't the father I could have been. What a great lesson . . . the only way I could begin to learn it was on my knees. If she had said those things to my face I would have suspected her of trying a new approach to get her own way.

The key to a successful marriage is not doing things for each other, it's doing things *with* each other. It's not getting old together, it's *growing* old together. It's not acting like a husband and wife are supposed to act, it's spending your lives learning to *be* what a husband and wife should be.

My friend, it'll hurt. It'll cost. Lots of young people think marriage is a honeymoon. A honeymoon? It's warfare! But we're both winning now that I'm learning what it means to be a husband. I'm glad I didn't give up on her and she didn't give up on me, because we're changing just enough to learn what it is to make the marriage decision ours and to die by it — that's *real living*.

WHAT ARE YOU GOING TO LIVE YOUR LIFE IN?

Some people say a person misses success because he doesn't have sufficient aptitude. Actually, aptitude has little to do with success. The success of a person in business or any other endeavor is never determined by aptitude, by the boss or by friends. Success is achieved through making a decision, making it yours and dying by it.

I'll never forget when the manager gave me basic training in Harrisburg. He told me about the job's freedom and success and prestige and how I'd laugh my way to the bank. "Brother," I thought, "how long has this been going on?" I thought the people would break my door down when they found out what I was selling. What did I discover when I went into the field? The manager had lied; at least he exaggerated.

Well, I was going to quit, but I couldn't afford postage to mail in my resignation. Sometimes I wrote down why I was going to quit, but I was so ashamed of the shabby reason I didn't go through with it. When I got a better reason I couldn't think of a real reason, so I stuck it out.

Later, when I was a manager, I realized some of the personnel thought they didn't have a good leader. I'd say, "All right, I know you deserve a better leader than I am, but I'm all you have and I'm not quitting. If you don't cooperate, you're going to put up with me the rest of your life." We had beautiful cooperation!

Did you ever watch a man picking out a job? Let's watch this man coming into the employment office.

"Hello, Mr. Manager, I would like to try out your business. I've seen some of your guys that aren't very good even on the coffee break. I'd like to try out this business, and if I like it I'll stay on."

One's life work, I have learned, grows with the working and living. Do it as if your life depended on it, and first thing you know you'll have made a life out of it. A good life, too.
—Theresa Helburn

The poor manager is so hard up for help these days he's just likely to say: "Sign up."

Now, that's like my going to my wife before we were married and saying, "Hello there, sugar, I've been watching your style. I'd like to try you and if I like you I'll keep you."

You can't try out a woman and make a marriage, and you can't try out a job and make a career. Unless you're willing to commit yourself to a company and learn to be an employee in the same way you commit yourself to a partner and learn to be a spouse, you're doomed to fail before you start.

You say, "Well, I didn't do it that way and I've been hanging on." Yes, there are a lot of failures who never quit!

Let's look at a more sophisticated shopper. "Hello there, Mr. Manager. I've been all over town and interviewed five companies. Your name has come up a couple of times as being pretty good. Before I make my big decision about coming with a company, I want you to tell me what you have to offer. If you have a better deal than these other five, you're going to get *me*."

That's something like my going to a woman and saying, "Hello there, honey. You know, I've been lookin' at ya. I've got five other cuties on the string, but I'm not making any decision until I know what you have to offer me. If you shape up, you're going to get *me*."

Brother, if she gets me she won't get much, will she? And the company who gets a man on the basis of what it can give him isn't going to get much. A lot of men never get to know the thrill of letting a job make them what they ought to be because they don't start right.

I've never seen a man who was a failure on his job and was good for anything else. I've been learning that a job is something God gives to me and says that I'm to walk worthy of the vocation wherewith I've been called, that I'm to begin learning to do everything I can with all my heart. If a man isn't learning to love, honor and cherish his job, it will never honor him and reward him any more than a self-centered marriage will.

Of course, an employee should know what future benefits a company offers, but they shouldn't have priority. The deal a company offers is important, but not as important as the relationships. The pay is important, but the opportunities to give and grow are more important.

Many people will miss the privilege of growing up and growing old on a great team because they missed on this great decision. A job is like a marriage: you can court several favorites, but until you settle down with one you'll miss real success in a career or a marriage. You must commit your life to a partner or career in order to grow and glow. The key to vocational success is not proper training, aptitude, or "pull" with the boss, but making the job decision, making it yours and dying by it.

WHAT ARE YOU GOING TO LIVE YOUR LIFE FOR?

The third big decision is: What are you going to live your life for? There are only two things to live your life for. I won't spend much time on the first because we're all authorities on it. The first thing that we live our lives for is the big I, me, mine. "Hey, world, look at me; ain't I terrific! I'm a self-made man!" (Good, that relieves God of the responsibility!) We can't fool each other; we all recognize the guy who makes the sun rise and set on his wonderful pinhead!

Yes, I can live my life for me . . . or I can live it for God.

"Oh-oh, we don't talk about religion," someone says. "That causes controversy." Yes, that's true. But sometimes controversy sheds new light.

Now, I want to make it clear I'm not talking about gaining success by following God. You've probably heard somebody say, "Do you want to be a success? Get religion." If you want success, don't do that! I know some of the finest spiritual people who have nothing materially, and I know some of the shrewdest con men who have all the material success one could want. So we can't equate knowing God with financial success.

Neither do I believe God solves all our problems. In fact, I believe he gives us bigger and better ones! When people come to know God, life will not get easier, but it will get *better*. If good baseball players want to play against good opponents, and tough football players want to play tough competitors, don't living people want to *live* instead of vegetate? Conflict, striving, sacrificing — not ease and rest — make real men and women!

A fellow said to me, "Charlie, are you one of these guys who believe other people ought to believe because you believe?" No, I don't believe that. Another guy said, "Do you believe that people should believe all that you believe?" I said, "No, but I do believe that a person ought to know what he believes, why he believes it and then *believe* it."

I remember a meeting in Palm Springs that attracted some thirty men who had done about five hundred million dollars' worth of business the year before. Our speaker couldn't tell us much about selling and recruiting, but he said something that arrested my attention: "Men, you're not ready to live your life until you know what you want written on your tombstone." I thought, "Hmmm, I'll need a big monument. . . ." No, he wasn't talking about the monument. He meant simply: What are you living your life for? — although he used different words.

Religion was one of the things I was always against. I was against religion because I just didn't believe in living with a prop or crutch, and another reason was that I was *for* what religion was *agin*.

When I was a young man, church people would say to me: "Jones, you should hate sin." I thought, "I love it! I've never had a sin lesson in my life; it came natural to me."

My dad used to say, "Now, look here, son, you've got to quit drinking, smoking, swearing, and gambling." I'd say, "Wait a minute, Dad. I might as well go to hell now — what am I going to do with all my time?"

Somebody else would tell me: "You've got to get religion." I'd say, "Wait a minute. I'm happier without religion than you are with it. If you want to work on somebody, why don't you work on some of those miserable religious people and

Nothing in life can compare with the thrill of knowing God and knowing he knows you.
—C. E. J.

let me be happy?" That would scare them off.

I remember someone saying to me: "You've got to do the best you can to make it through." I'd say, "The best I can? My friend, if doing the best I can is the criterion for getting to heaven, then I'm a cinch for hell because I never did the best I could one day in my life." I always could have done a little better if I'd tried a little harder. So I must have been going to hell in style — along with everybody else who was failing to do the best they could.

Then one day they told me, "Jones, you've got to get your children baptized or they won't make it to heaven." I thought, "Hmmm, I can take a chance on my own fate but I shouldn't take a chance on my children." So some eighteen years ago we all stood before a huge group of people and were baptized. I can still remember how sick I felt about all those promises I made to the pastor. Would I do such and such, he asked. And I said, "Yes, yes, yes." I knew I was lying every time, but all my buddies had lied and I figured I didn't have any right to upset the applecart this late in the game.

Then one day I was driving along when I saw a fellow I hadn't seen for years. I stopped and he jumped in my car. That was a miracle; most people were jumping out! I was ready to sell, but he took the play away from me. "Charlie Jones, how is it with your soul?" he said.

I said, "My what?"

He said, "Are you born again?"

I thought, "Here I am."

He said, "Are you going to heaven when you die?"

"When I die!" I said, "I'm just getting revved up now to live!"

This fellow whipped out his Bible, and I realized that for the first time in my life I had encountered a religious fanatic — but he sure looked healthy. Carefully I set about my strategy. I always let the prospect talk himself out, and when he's talked out I would solve his problem. The only trouble with this fellow was that he never shut up.

Well, he trapped me. I was all set to give him my Sunday punches but he wouldn't hold still. I knew all the religious cliches and the answers, but this guy didn't tell me what church to join, what to quit, or what to buy. He told me that the Bible is true, that Jesus Christ is man's Savior and that God loves sinners.

I thought God loved only religious people, and here I heard that he loves scoundrels. But I couldn't believe it. I said, "You mean to tell me that God loves me and wants to come into my life, just like that? Are you trying to start a new religion? You come along and tell me to do nothing but surrender my heart and let God live in my life. I've listened to a lot of religious discussions but this is the first time I've heard that."

He said, "Maybe it's because . . ." and he read me something from the Bible. I'd read every book I could to disprove the Bible. I figured the

Bible was a myth, a fable, a literary classic. I told him, "It's only for the ignoramuses and the poverty-stricken. It's not for people who *know*." But he just kept reading Scripture that I couldn't answer.

I said, "All right, when I'm ready to turn over a new leaf I'll get some of this; it sounds good."

He said, "You don't need a new leaf; you need a new life."

I thought, "Wonder how he knew that!"

I soon saw he wasn't going to buy any insurance, and I didn't want to be converted. And so I got ready to usher him out of my car. He knew he was fighting a rear-guard action now, but he stuck to his ground — quoting Scriptures I couldn't do anything with.

Finally he said, "All right, Charlie, I'm going to leave, but you remember this: if the Bible is wrong and you're right, the Christians have nothing to lose. But if the Bible is right and you're wrong, you have everything to lose." Then he said, "The Protestant, Jew and Catholic disagree on a lot of things, but they agree on this: the Bible is the Word of God."

That was the best case for Christianity I'd ever heard. I got rid of him, but I couldn't forget him. I made up my mind right then I'd not eat another meal, I'd not sell another policy, I'd not talk to another person until I determined if this were true. If the Bible were not true, then I would throw it in the trash can, sleep on Sunday mornings and save my dollar a week. But if I decided that the Bible is true, I would ask God to make me a Christian no matter what it takes or whatever a Christian is.

I knew I didn't need God to be successful. I didn't need God to be an American. I didn't need God to get a wife. I didn't need God to have children. But I did need something.

As I look back now, I realize I never knew what it was to be loved in the true sense of the word. I had never felt love penetrate beyond the barriers that we all set up in our hearts. I didn't know then that such love existed.

So I drove the streets that day in Lancaster and pondered. I remembered another startling thing my friend had said: "Charlie, there's nothing you can do for God; God wants to do it all for you."

That was a new approach. People used to come to me and say, "God could use a guy like you." My answer was: "If God needs *me* to help him out, he's in too much trouble already."

After much thinking, I stopped my car and bowed my head and said, "Now, God, I don't understand all this, but somehow for the first time I believe the Bible is true and I'm a sinner. I want you to forgive me and come into my heart

---

My most cherished possession I wish I could leave you is my faith in Jesus Christ, for with him and nothing else you can be happy, but without him and with all else you'll never be happy. —*Patrick Henry*

and make me whatever a Christian is, in Christ's name, Amen."

I raised my head after saying "Amen" and waited for the angels' wings to flap or the stars to burst. I had heard about getting religion and I thought, "Whoooo, this is going to be great now." I sat there, and not a thing happened!

I thought, "Maybe God thinks I'm praying one of my old style prayers." I used to pray often and I'd say, "Lord, let me get hot today and clean up, and I'll turn over a new leaf." But they weren't prayers. Now, for the first time in my life, I was praying an honest prayer from the depths of my heart.

I bowed my head again like a child and said, "Now, Lord, I really mean business. Hear my prayer. Amen."

I raised my head again. Still no feeling. And it didn't come the rest of that day — or the next day! But I realized something.

As a boy I wanted to grow up and be a man. I could hardly wait to know what it is to feel like a man. At twelve I'd slip into the bathroom after my father was finished shaving and I'd get out the old straight razor and mug. They had told me that if I shaved off the peach fuzz the whiskers would jump out sooner — wow, that's what I needed to feel like a man.

I used to put on my dad's shoes and hold his pants against me to see if I were gaining on him. When I was twenty years and three hundred sixty-four days old, I could hardly wait one more day to feel like a real, live, red-blooded *man*. And then came my twenty-first birthday, and I didn't feel a bit different!

I could hardly wait to know what it was like to be married. I knew why I didn't feel right when she accepted my marriage proposal — I didn't have her signed, sealed and delivered. When I had someone who belonged to me completely, I knew I'd feel like whatever it was I was missing.

Then I stood before the preacher and he said, "I now pronounce you man and wife." There, I had her. But I didn't feel a bit different. A few weeks later, if I had rolled over in bed and said, "Dear, I don't feel married anymore," she'd have said, "You are, just the same, and don't you try to get out of it!"

There was no use denying I was married. I had accepted her and she had accepted me, and we were married. I never had to feel it. But I'd better believe it!

One day I quit being proud of being against God and made a decision to ask him into my life. God said he would come in, I believe it, and that settled it.

Don't you live your life flying by the seat of your pants. Disregard feelings. That indulgence is only for those who live by whims. The person who's learning to really live will know what it is to make a decision and stick by it.

When you make a decision make it *yours*. *Live for it.* Burn that into your heart. Remember, *decisions aren't to make men; men are to make decisions.*

My Before-
and After-Thoughts

My best lessons in life are not those teaching me new things so much as those helping me unlearn some old things.

A sure-fire growth formula: cram fifty years of failure into fifteen.

Life's greatest challenge is not being a man's man but God's man.

A company's goal should not be getting more men into their business or getting more of their business into the men; the great challenge is to get more man into a man.

Don't worry about being of more use where you aren't; the best job you'll ever have is the one you're on. No job ever made a man but a right man can make any job.

A man is never a failure until he blames someone else.

It's not important that everyone is like you, but it's very important that there is someone just like you.

Don't spend your life trying to make right decisions; invest your life in making decisions and making them right.

— *Charles "T" Jones*

4

Leaders Are Readers

One of the greatest thoughts I've ever heard is, "You will be the same in five years as you are today except for the people you meet and the books you read." You know, that's absolutely true.

Several years ago someone gave me a copy of *Wake up and Live*. Boy, what a book! Written by a woman, too! I have nothing against women, you understand, but it's amazing that this is better than what any man could write — it proves that we're at least equal after all!

This book is great because it excitingly tells how to be a success. One discouraging discovery for me was that I am doing more to fail than I am to succeed. Someone asked me, "If you're doing more to fail than to succeed, how come you're so successful?" I don't claim any credit;

can I help it if other people are trying harder to fail than I am?

Tell me: what is it that makes us fail? Anxiety, fear, uncertainty, insecurity, selfishness, jealousy, thanklessness, irritability, disorganization . . . do you think I ever took a course in those? I'm tremendous in all of them. They come naturally to me.

But what does it take to be real, to grow? It takes courage, warmth, depth, sincerity, faith, thankfulness, selflessness . . . I lack by nature everything that it takes to be successful. I can act it out, sure, but sometimes when a guy's learned to be an actor he gets the rug pulled out from under him.

I don't want to be an actor nor a failure, but I need help. Books have helped me to think about things and frame some tremendous thoughts that I would never have come near without reading.

I'll never forget the thrill I got when I read a book filled with tremendous truths that were completely opposite to what I had believed. After the first book, I found a string of them, and many of these terrific insights were first written fifty to one hundred years ago.

I began to share these ideas by buying the books in quantity and giving a book to everyone who came in my office. If they didn't want to read — they got one anyway. I knew they would get an impulse sometime to read, and these books could do more for them than a truckload of pills.

The books began to change my life and the lives of my friends and associates. Then I realized I had overlooked the most important people in my life, my family. My oldest son Jere was 14 years old at the time. He was a perfect example of the modern teenager. He never did anything wrong; he never did anything right; he just never did anything! Oh, he fooled around at sports. He made the school honor roll. But when it came to sparkle he was dead. He was such an introvert that he couldn't even lead in silent prayer!

I — like most dads — have been critical of the way they do things in Washington, but one day I realized I was running a worse program in my home than the politicians in government. I decided it was time for a change, and since books had been so tremendously helpful in my life I decided to use them with my son.

I knew Jere would rebel against my forcing him to read, so I planned some strategy. You know, you can take a horse to water, but you can't make him drink — well, I decided to put some salt in Jere's oats and make him thirsty.

"Jere, in two years you're going to want me to help you buy a car, and I want to help you. But I'm not going to give you the money. Here is my proposal. I'm going to pay you $10 for every book you read. I'll pick the book, you give me a written report, and I'll put $10 in a car fund. So, if you read in style, you'll drive in style. But if you read like a bum, you'll drive like a bum." Overnight he developed a tremendous hunger for reading!

The first book I gave him was Dale Carnegie's *How To Win Friends and Influence People.* I'll never forget his coming down the staircase the next day with a big smile and saying, "Dad, there is a whole chapter in there on smiling and shaking hands!" And he was smiling at me — at only 14 years of age! I've known some men who go most of their life without learning to smile and give a vigorous handshake!

The next book I had him read was *The Atom Speaks,* by D. Lee Chesnut. Chesnut was a sales manager for General Electric, and his book tied the spiritual and scientific strands of life together. I had him read this because I knew when he went off to college there was a chance he'd write home the usual "Dear Dad" letter:

Dear Dad,

Your faith isn't relevant. I don't believe in your God. Goodbye.

I wanted to make sure that when he went off to college, he didn't go with my faith in God, but his faith in God, and if his didn't work it was *his* fault. No kid can make his parents' faith work; he has to have his own. I also wanted to prepare him for the professor who might try to prove God unnecessary.

One only reads well when one reads with some quite personal goal in mind.
— Paul Valery

My heart aches for the boy whose dad sends him off for an education before teaching him a little of the why and how of living. I like what one leading executive said: "After spending a lifetime in management development, I'm convinced that spiritual growth is more important than education; you can get an education and not grow, but you can't help getting an education if you grow spiritually."

I'll never forget giving Jere a book by Alan Redpath, a pastor in England. It's about the life of Joshua in the Bible. This book makes the Old Testament come alive. It teaches you how you can lose in *style!* I told Jere, "Live to win, but when you lose, wow! enjoy it and get on to the next battle." Jere never could understand that until I gave him Redpath's book.

An illustration in this book describes two pastors meeting on the street. One pastor says to the other, "Hey, I heard you had a great revival at your church."

He said, "We sure did."

"How many additions did you have?"

"None, but we sure had some blessed subtractions!"

You see, you don't have to *get* in order to win; sometimes you lose and win. Well, we were going to Sunday school and I said, "Jere, how are you getting along with my friend Alan Redpath?"

Jere looked over and said, "Dad, everybody ought to read that book." And then he reached over and whacked my leg and said, "No, Dad,

everybody ought to *have* to read that book!"
Fifteen years my boy had lain around my house
practically dead, and now he had a tiger in his
think-tank!

Jere eventually read twenty-two books. Did
he buy the car? No, he kept the money and used
my car and my gas. Did he write a "Dear Dad"
letter? Yes and no. He wrote me a "Dear Dad"
card every day after he went to college, but the
words thrilled me. He made a habit of writing
every day about a new idea that had hit him, or
a fresh slant on an old idea. And these ideas
have come from his reading. I can tell you the
very page of the book that I paid him to read
which inspired some of these tremendous ideas!

Here are a few of Jere's notes that show what
books did for him — and his dad!

Dear Dad,
   The only happy man, successful man, confi-
dent man or practical man is the one who is sim-
ple. SIB-KIS.* Unless his mind can crystalize
all the answers into one powerful punch of per-
sonal motivation, he will live nothing but a life of
uncertainty and fear.
(*See It Big — Keep It Simple)

                              Tremendously, too (Tt),
                                        Jere

Dad,
   It is tremendous to be able to know that when
you are in a slump, just as the baseball player
will break out in time, so you will break out of

yours. Yes, time really cures things. Like you said, you don't lose any problems, you just get bigger and better ones. Tremendous ones!

Tt,
Jere

Dad,

Just started reading 100 Great Lives. Thanks for what you said in the front — the part that every great man never sought to be great; he just followed the vision he had and did what had to be done!

Love,
Jere

Dad,

I just got done typing up little quotes out of the Bible and Napoleon (Hill) so that everywhere I I look I see them. When people ask what they are, I will tell them. They are my pin-ups.

Jere

Dad,

I am more convinced than ever that you can do anything you want; you can beat anyone at anything, just by working hard. Handicaps don't mean anything because often people who don't have them have a bad attitude and don't want to work.

Jere

Dad,

Nothing new, just the same old exciting thought

that we can know God personally and forever in this amazing life!

Jere

Dad,

The mind of God is so unbelievable. He throws nothing but paradoxes at us. He makes us completely and utterly helpless and depraved; and then takes that failure which normally knocks us out — and makes it our greatest asset.

Jere

Dad,

When you're behind two papers in the fourth quarter, and you are exhausted from the game, and you have to make this set of downs in order to stay in the game, and you get up to the line and see five 250-lb. tests staring you in the mug, it sure is exciting to wait to find out what play the Lord will call next! WOW!

Jere

Now you know why I believe in the power of books! I like to share good things, and so I relate some of these experiences to groups around the country. In New Orleans a man came up to me and said he had started his son on a reading program after hearing me speak in Dallas, and he was enthusiastic about the results.

"I'm a better salesman than you are," he greeted me. "How so?" I asked. "I got my kid reading for only five bucks a book," he said.

Then he added: "If I had known ahead of time what these books would do for my boy, I would have been glad to pay $100 a book! I'd even go to $1,000 a book — except that we have six children!"

When people began asking the names of the books Jere had read, I printed a list of the titles and distributed thousands of copies. Later I decided that the best way to introduce different types of readers to inspirational books was to compile sets of outstanding paperbacks to meet particular needs and interests. I put the books into "power packs" for leaders, salesmen, wives, teenagers, church workers and mothers, and offered them at a nominal amount. I guarantee that anyone who is reading these books steadily will experience a constant personal revolution.

Space won't permit much illustration of the books' contents, but I'd like to highlight a few of the thoughts from the Power Packs that have meant so much to the Joneses. (See page 107 for publishers' data.)

How To Win Over Worry, by John Haggai

For your own peace of mind excel in at least one thing. Concentrate all your forces upon work. Gather in your resources, rally all your faculties, marshal all your energies, focus all your capacities upon mastery in at least one field of endeavor. This is a "sure-fire" antidote to the divided mind. Stop scattering your fire. Cease any half-hearted interests to be superb in everything. Ascertain the will of the Lord for your life. Enlist his help and strength through whom you can do all things. Strive for the mastery — and experience worry-killing poise through skill.

The Reason Why, by Robert A. Laidlaw

Suppose that a young man should send his fiancée a diamond costing him $500, placing it in a little case which the jeweler threw in for nothing. How disappointed he would be if, when meeting her a few days later, she said, "Darling, that was a lovely little box you sent me. In order to take special care of it, I promise to keep it wrapped up in a safe place so that no harm should come to it." Rather ridiculous, isn't it? Yet, it is just as foolish for men and women to be spending all their time and thought on their bodies, which are only cases containing the real self, the soul, which, the Bible tells us, will persist long after our bodies have crumbled to dust. The soul is of infinite value.

Psycho-Cybernetics, by Maxwell Maltz

We often overlook the fact that man too has a success instinct, much more marvelous and much more complex than that of any animal. Our Creator did not short-change man. On the other hand, man was especially blessed in this regard. Animals cannot select their goals. Their goals (self-preservation and procreation) are pre-set, so to speak. And their success mechanism is limited to these built-in goal-images, which we call "instincts."

Man, on the other hand, has something animals haven't — Creative Imagination. Thus man of all creatures is more than a creature, he is also a creator. With his imagination he can formulate a variety of goals. Man alone can direct his Success Mechanism by the use of imagination, or "imaging" ability.

(All of the above books are in the Leader's Power Pack.)

A Woman's World, by Clyde M. Narramore

You are an intelligent being. God has given you an inquiring mind. Yet, unless you are satisfying its demand for mental stimulation, you will become stale and uninteresting.

Intelligence is not a quality chiefly cornered by the male sex or by a few gifted women. Every person has intellectual qualities. Unfortunately, some women become so involved in the daily routine of the home or office that they squelch their intellectuality. The important factor is not merely what you learn, but also your own attitude toward self-development. When you see the value of continued growth, the circumstances around you can become stepping stones. Much of the knowledge you assimilate in life is gained in an informal manner. When you learn to sharpen your powers of discernment and train yourself to be more observant, a whole new world will unfold before you. Even the commonplace will take on new meaning.

Advice from a Failure, by Jo Coudert

Many people, if they were to treat other people as they treat their spouses, would soon have not a friend in the world. Why it is assumed that marriage is more impervious to the effects of discourtesy than friendship, I do not know, but of the people I have encountered, only head waiters, truck drivers, and married couples are consistently insulting. If I were to formulate a single banner to raise over marriage, it would be this: Love, let us be kind to each other.

(These are from two of the 13 potent books in the Wife's Power Pack.)

I Dare You, by William Danforth

H. G. Wells tells how every human being can determine whether he has really succeeded in life. He says: "Wealth, notoriety, place, and power are no measure of success whatever. The only true measure of success is the ratio between what we might have done and what we might have been on the one hand, and the thing we have made and the thing we have made of ourselves on the other."

I want you to start a crusade in your life

— to dare to be your best. I maintain that you are a better, more capable person than you have demonstrated so far. The only reason you are not the person you should be is you don't dare to be. Once you dare, once you stop drifting with the crowd and face life courageously, life takes on a new significance. New forces take shape within you.

Your God Is Too Small by J. B. Phillips

It appears that the strategy of Christ was to win the loyalty of the few who would honestly respond to the new way of living. They would be the pioneers of the new order, the spearhead of advance against the massed ignorance, selfishness, evil, "play-acting," and apathy of the majority of the human race. The goal which was set before them, for which they were to work and pray — and if need be, suffer and die — was the building of a new Kingdom of inner supreme loyalty, the Kingdom of God. This was to transcend every barrier of race and frontier and — this is important — of time and space as well.

Public Speaking, by Dale Carnegie

We have only four contacts with the world, you and I. We are evaluated and classified by four things: by what we do, by how we look, by what we say, and by how we say it. Yet many a person blunders through a long lifetime, after he leaves school, without any

conscious effort to enrich his stock of words,
to master their shades of meaning, to speak
with precision and distinction. He comes
habitually to use the overworked and exhausted phrases of the office and street.
Small wonder that his talk lacks distinction
and individuality.

(There are nine more life-changing books in
the Teenager's Power Pack.)

That Incredible Christian, by A. W. Tozer
The cross-carrying Christian, furthermore, is
both a confirmed pessimist and an optimist
the like of which is to be found nowhere else
on earth.

When he looks at the cross he is a pessimist, for he knows that the same judgment
that fell on the Lord of glory condemns in
that one act all nature and all the world of
men. He rejects every human hope out of
Christ because he knows that man's noblest
effort is only dust building on dust.

Yet he is calmly, restfully optimistic. If
the cross condemns the world, the resurrec-
tion of Christ guarantees the ultimate triumph
of good throughout the universe. Through
Christ all will be well at last and the Christian waits the consummation. Incredible
Christian!

The Release of the Spirit, by Watchman Nee
Anyone who serves God will discover sooner

or later that the great hindrance to his work is not others but himself. He will discover that his outward man and his inward man are not in harmony, for both are tending toward opposite directions. He will also sense the inability of his outward man to submit to the Spirit's control, thus rendering him incapable of obeying God's highest commands. He will quickly detect that the greatest difficulty lies in his outward man, for it hinders him from using his spirit.

(These books, like the 11 others in the Church Worker's Power Pack, go to the core of our problems and the center of God's solutions.)

A new set of books, the Family Power Pack, features *The Living New Testament* — the modern-language paraphrase, two illustrated teen editions of New Testament books and *Spirit-Controlled Temperament,* a uniquely practical book on personality and spiritual problems written by pastor-counselor Tim LaHaye.

Readers are not necessarily leaders, but leaders are almost always readers. The person who is paving the way or setting the pace can wear out or dry up mentally as well as physically because the mind needs food. The ten books in the Leader's Power Pack have been tremendously helpful to me as a father, husband, salesman, manager, citizen and servant. There are many more books that could be added to the list, but any five of these can make this project the most profitable of your life.

Pictures of these Power Packs and the names of the books appear at the end of this book. Cost-wise, every set is a bargain; vocationally and personally, every Power Pack is a solid investment in the future. We offer these books from Life Management Services because we believe they can make life exciting, satisfying, *tremendous!* I am convinced that the right books in the hands and hearts of rightly motivated people could turn their world right-side-up!

A cardinal rule to remember in reading inspirational books: You only get to keep and enjoy what you share and give away. If you aren't going to read with the purpose of sharing and giving, I suggest you give the books to someone who will share with you and you'll discover the power of books as you watch the reader grow through sharing with you. Perhaps the best idea would be to use the "brain trust" idea of "Think and Grow Rich" and both of you begin reading and sharing with each other.

Now — you've framed some vital thoughts through reading this book: you know you're a leader in one way or another; you know you're important to God and your fellowman; you know that the quality of life depends on observance of basic laws of the universe; you know (I trust) that life can be tremendous — so *jump in* — you were made for this swim!

How To Win Over Worry, by John Haggai, © 1959 by the author, published by Zondervan Publishing House, Grand Rapids, Mich. Used by permission.

The Reason Why, by Robert Laidlaw, published by Moody Press, Chicago, Ill. Used by permission.

Psycho-Cybernetics, by Maxwell Maltz, © 1960 Prentice-Hall, Inc., N.Y., N.Y. Used by permission.

A Woman's World, by Clyde Narramore, © 1963 Zondervan Publishing House, Grand Rapids, Mich. Used by permission.

Advice from a Failure, by Jo Coudert, © 1965 by the author, published by Stein and Day, Inc., N.Y., N.Y. Paperback by Dell Publ. Co., N.Y., N.Y. Used by permission.

I Dare You, by William Danforth, © 1967 The American Youth Foundation, St. Louis, Mo. Used by permission.

Your God Is Too Small, by J. B. Phillips, © The Macmillan Company, N.Y., N.Y. Used by permission.

Public Speaking, by Dale Carnegie, © 1956 National Board of Young Men's Christian Associations, N.Y., N.Y. Used by permission of Association Press. Paperback edition published by Dell Pub. Co. 1956.

That Incredible Christian, by A. W. Tozer, © 1964 Christian Publications, Inc., Harrisburg, Pa. Used by permission.

The Release of the Spirit, by Watchman Nee, © 1965 Sure Foundation.

Life's Great Thoughts

The man is no fool who gives up what he can't keep to gain what he can't lose.
— *Jim Elliot*

Sense shines with a double luster when it is set in humility. An able and yet humble man is a jewel worth a kingdom.
— *William Penn*

The man who has no more problems to solve is out of the game. — *Elbert Hubbard*

There are two brands of discontent: the brand that merely fosters greed and snarling and back-biting, and the brand that inspires greater and greater effort to reach the desired goal. What is your brand? — *B. C. Forbes*

We learn wisdom from failure much more than from success. We often discover what will do by finding out what will not do, and probably he who never made a mistake never made a discovery. — *Samuel Smiles*

If you have a weakness, make it work for you as a strength — and if you have a strength, don't abuse it into a weakness.
— *Dore Schary*

The great thing in the world is not so much where we stand as in what direction we are moving. —*Oliver Wendell Holmes*

Difficulties are things that show what men are. —*Epictetus*

I must confess that I'm driven to my knees by the overwhelming conviction that I have nowhere else to go. My wisdom and that of all about me is insufficient to meet the demands of the day. —*Lincoln*

Unfortunately, we are too inclined to talk of man as it would be desirable for him to be rather than as he really is. True education can proceed only from naked reality, not from any ideal illusion about man, however attractive. —*Carl Jung*

What a man knows should find its expression in what he does; the value of superior knowledge is chiefly in that it leads to a performing manhood. —*Christian Bovee*

Great opportunities come to all, but many do not know they have met them. The only preparation to take advantage of them is simple fidelity to what each day brings. —*A. E. Dunning*

In great attempts it is glorious even to fail. —*Longinus*

The man of true greatness never loses his child's heart. — *Mencius*

When you are no longer in danger of being thought of as a hypocrite by your friends, beware of your hypocrisy with God.
— *Oswald Chambers*

LEADER'S POWER PACK

The Reason Why . . . . Laidlaw
World Aflame . . . . Graham
Wake Up and Live . . . . Brande
Man's Seach for Meaning . . . . Frankl
How to Win Friends and
   Influence People . . . . Carnegie
How to Live 365
   Days a Year . . . . Schindler
Good News . . . . Phillips
How to Win Over Worry . . . . . Haggai
The Goal and the Glory . . . Simonson
Think and Grow Rich . . . . Hill
Living Letters . . . . Taylor
The Great Quotations . . . . Seldes
Psycho - Cybernetics . . . . Maltz

WIFE'S POWER PACK

The Greatest Thing in
   the World . . . . Drummond
How to Stop Worrying and
   Start Living . . . . Carnegie
Always Ask a Man . . . . Dahl
Henrietta Mears and How
   She Did It . . . . . . Baldwin, Benson
None of These Diseases . . . . McMillen
Look Younger, Live Longer . . . Houser
Christian's Secret of a
   Happy Life . . . . Smith
In His Steps . . . . Sheldon
Advice from a Failure . . . . Coudert
A Woman's World . . . . Narramore
A Woman's Choice . . . . Price
The Ability to Love . . . . Fromme
How To Live with Yourself
   and Like It . . . . Lindgren

TEENAGER'S POWER PACK

How to Develop Self Confidence and Influence
   People by Public Speaking . . . . . . Carnegie
New Ways to Greater Word Power . . Goodman,
                                     Lewin
Sometimes I Feel Like a Blob . . . . . . Barrett
How to Be a Christian Without
   Being Religious . . . . Ridenour
Your God is Too Small . . . . Phillips
The Heart of a Champion . . . . Richards
Profiles in Courage . . . . Kennedy
I Dare You . . . . Danforth
I Loved a Girl . . . . Trobisch
Get Smart . . . . Taylor
Come Alive . . . . Taylor
Love and the Facts of Life . . . . Duvall

CHURCH WORKER'S POWER PACK

FAMILY POWER PACK

Life Management Services
P.O. Box 1044
Harrisburg, Pa. 17108